Contents

Josh   *Con*

CHAPTER 1

Olympic Shampoo Star

Best friends Con and Josh are sitting in Con's living room, watching the Olympic Games on television.

Con "I'd love to be an Olympic champion."

Josh "Me too."

Con "What events would you do?"

Josh "All of them!"

Con "As if. If you did that, you'd be the greatest and most famous sportsman in the world."

Josh "Yes, how cool would that be? I'd be on every TV ad selling stuff like shampoo."

Con "Yes, I can see it now. 'Hi, my name is Josh. I won every gold medal at the last Olympic Games, but I couldn't have done it without my extra soft and silky shampoo.'"

Josh (laughing) "And you too can run, jump and swim like me if you wash your hair with this shampoo."

Con "Hey, do you want to have our own Olympics?"

Josh "Yes! Where? How?"
Con "Follow me."

Con and Josh head outside into Con's back garden.

Con "This will be our Olympic Stadium!"

Josh "What? You mean your
back garden?"

Con "Yes! So, are you ready for the
first event?"

Josh "Bring it on! The world is
about to see a new Olympic
legend!"

CHAPTER 2

The Events

Before they start, the boys decide to set the ground rules for the contest.

Con "So we'll do four events. Whoever wins the most will win the gold medal. Okay?"

Josh "Yes. Got it."

Con "Right, the first event will be the shot-put. We'll use this old brick here."

Josh "Cool. I want to represent Great Britain."

Con "No, I do!"

Josh "I said it first. Pick another country."

Con "No, how about we make up
our own countries. Just to make
it fair."

Josh "Okay. My country is called ...
um ... 'the United States of Josh',
or 'USJ'. And my flag would have
a picture of me and lots of stars
around it."

Con "Cool. Well, my country is called 'Conland'. And my flag would have lots of stripes and a big 'C' in the middle of it."

Josh "Okay. Well, I'll throw the shot-put first."

Josh picks up the brick and tosses it. It lands in the middle of the back garden.

Josh "*And what a wonderful throw by the Joshican. The USJ has a history of winning this event. But can they do it again? It looks like it was a 2.2 metre throw.*"

Josh marks his spot with an old bus ticket he happens to have in his pocket. He returns the brick to Con.

Con *"Now it's time for the great Con. Conland has never won this event before but things could change here at this magnificent stadium. And the crowd hold their breath ... "*

Josh "Just throw it, will you!"

Con *"And he takes his run up ... "*

Con tosses the brick with all
his might.

Con *"And look at it go! It looks like
it's going to be the winning throw*
… Oh no, it's heading straight for
Mum's garden gnome … "

Smash!

CHAPTER 3

The Next Contest

Con and Josh run up to the gnome—
it's smashed into several pieces. Con
rushes inside and returns with some
superglue.

Josh "What did your mum say?"

Con "I wasn't going to tell her, but she saw me with the glue in my hand. She told me not to worry too much 'cause she was thinking of getting rid of it anyway."

Josh "So why do you want to bother trying? Forget it. I won that event. We've got to do the next one now."

Con "What do you mean you won? My throw went further than yours!"

Josh "Yeah, but you hit one of the Olympic officials outside the marked area. So you're disqualified."

Con "Fine, then. Let's do the next event. The triple jump."

Con and Josh head to the top of the back garden. Con then rushes over to the shed and returns with an old mattress.

Con "We can use this to land on.
I'll put it here. Now, we use most
of the back garden to run, hop,
step and then jump onto the
mattress. Got it?"

Josh "Yes, Mr. President of the
Olympics! You can go first
this time."

Con takes his run. He hops, steps, jumps and then lands on the old mattress with a thud. He marks where he's landed with a leaf. Now it's Josh's turn. Josh sprints for the mattress and forgets to do the hop and step part. He jumps and flies right over the mattress, landing on the grass.

Josh "AARRGHH!"

Con runs to him.

Con "You hurt?"
Josh "No, I think I landed in something."

Josh stands up to find that he's landed on dog mess.

CHAPTER 4

Your Jump Stinks

Con breaks out laughing.

Josh "It's not funny! You should pick up your dog's mess."

Con "I do! But I can't help it if he just did one—I didn't see him do it because we were competing in the shot-put event."

Josh "I stink!"

Con "Yes, and so did your jump. You didn't hop or step, so you're disqualified. That makes me the winner of that event. That's 1 all."

Josh "Great—whatever! Do you have a spare pair of shorts for me? This smell is going to make me ill."

Josh follows Con inside Con's house and a few minutes later returns wearing a clean pair of shorts.

Josh "It was nice of your mum to
offer to wash my shorts. And to
give us these fizzy drinks."

Josh and Con are at the far end of
the garden, leaning against the back
fence, both bathed in sunshine.

Con "Yes, now we're Olympic champions, we need all the energy we can get, especially now that the score is even. The next event is going to be awesome between Conland and USJ."

Josh "So what is it?"

Con "Um ... "

Josh suddenly burps. A few
seconds later, Con does one too.

Con "That's it! That's our next
event. See who can burp the
longest."

CHAPTER 5

Neck and Neck

Josh and Con discuss whether burping should be an Olympic event.

Con "I think it should be, and since this is our Olympics, we can choose the events we want. You can go first. I'll time you. I'll use my watch as a stopwatch. Ready. Set. Go!"

Josh lets out an enormous,
rumbling burp.

Con "Cool! That was 2.13 seconds."
Josh "Okay. Your go. Give me your
watch. Ready. Set. Go!"

This time Con burps heavily.

Josh "Awrrh, I don't believe it!
You just beat me. Your time was
2.22 seconds."

Con "Yes! I only need to win
the next event and I win the
gold medal."

Josh "Okay. Let's make the next event gymnastics."

Con "Gymnastics?"

Josh "Yes, it's sort of gymnastics. We'll see how long we can do a handstand. We'll start together and the one who stays up the longest is the winner."

Con and Josh perform their handstands—their legs poking high in the air. Suddenly, Con's dog rushes over to him and begins to lick his face—making him lose his balance and topple over.

Josh "Yes, and the USJ wins!"

Con "That wasn't fair! I had interference."

Josh "It still counts. I can't help it if a crazy fan from the crowd ran out into the middle of the stadium and kissed you. So, that makes it even. We've won two events each."

Con "Does that mean we both win the gold medal?"

Con's mother calls out to the boys. "The hundred metre sprint is about to begin!"

Con and Josh shoot a look to each other.

Con "You thinking what I'm thinking?"

Josh "Yes. This will be the deciding event."

Con "First one to the living room wins the gold. Ready. Set. GO!!!!!!!!!!!!!!!!!"

equestrian events The horse riding events at the Olympic Games.

Olympic medals When you come first in an Olympic event you get a gold medal. When you come second you get a silver medal and when you come third you get a bronze medal.

opening ceremony A special party held at a stadium to welcome the athletes and to officially begin the Olympic Games.

triple jump A track and field event that is divided into three parts—hop, step and jump.

BOYS RULE!

Olympic Must-dos

☞ Train really hard if you want to be an Olympic star.

☞ Eat fresh, healthy foods such as fruit and vegetables. They'll give you plenty of energy.

☞ Drink plenty of water before and after your race.

☞ Go to bed early. Olympic stars need to rest their muscles.

☞ Try to beat your personal times.

☞ Respect the other competitors. You're all in the same boat—you love your sport.

☞ Send a fan letter to anyone who's ever made it to the Olympic Games. Not just to the winners either. You're a winner already if you've been picked to represent your country.

☞ Make your country's flag and wave it proudly. Pretend that you're in the opening ceremony.

☞ Learn the words to your national anthem—and sing it proudly in front of your family.

BOYS RULE!

Olympic
Instant Info

The Olympic Games are held every four years.

Great Britain has held the Olympic Games twice, both times in London. The first time was in 1908 and the second time was in 1948.

The first Olympic Games were recorded to have taken place in 776 BC. That was almost 3000 years ago.

Greece is the birthplace of the Olympic Games.

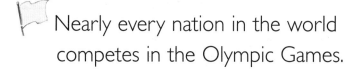 Nearly every nation in the world competes in the Olympic Games.

Greg Louganis from America holds the record for the most Olympic medals won in diving. He won five from 1976 to 1988.

The youngest person to win an athletics Olympic gold medal is American Barbara Jones, who was a runner in the US relay team at the 1952 Olympic Games. She was 15 years and 123 days old.

BOYS RULE!

Think Tank

1 Why do athletes have spikes on the bottom of their runners?

2 What do you do in the triple jump?

3 How far do you run in a 1500 metre race?

4 What is a stadium?

5 What colour medal do you win if you come first?

6 Where were the first Olympic Games held?

7 Is burping an official Olympic event?

8 Where were the 2004 Olympic Games held?

Answers

8 The 2004 Olympic Games were held in Athens, Greece.

7 No, burping isn't an official event, but it should be.

6 The first Olympic Games were held in Greece.

5 You win a gold medal for coming first.

4 It is where the main events of the Olympic Games are held.

3 You run 1500 metres. But that depends on whether you run all the way.

2 You do a hop, step and jump in the triple jump.

1 Athletes wear spikes to stop them from slipping over.

How did you score?

- If you got all 8 answers correct, then you've dreamed at least once in your life of making it to the Olympic Games.

- If you got 6 answers correct, then you like to watch the Olympics on television, but sometimes flick to the other channels.

- If you got fewer than 4 answers correct, then you like to watch the Olympics on television, but probably prefer to watch cartoons instead.

Felice → ← Phil

Hi Guys!

We have heaps of fun reading and want you to, too. We both believe that being a good reader is really important and so cool.

Try out our suggestions to help you have fun as you read.

At school, why don't you use "Olympic Champions" as a play and you and your friends can be the actors. Set the scene for your play. Use your imagination and pretend you're in the shot-put event. If you use something to throw, just make sure there's no-one in your way.

So ... have you decided who is going to be Con and who is going to be Josh? Now, with your friends, read and act out our story in front of the class.

We have a lot of fun when we go to schools and read our stories. After we finish the kids all clap really loudly. When you've finished your play your classmates will do the same. Just remember to look out the window—there might be a talent scout from a television station watching you!

Reading at home is really important and a lot of fun as well.

Take our books home and get someone in your family to read them with you. Maybe they can take on a part in the story.

Remember, reading is a whole lot of fun.

So, as the frog in the local pond would say, Read-it!

And remember, Boys Rule!

BOYS RULE!
When We Were Kids

Felice

Phil

Phil "Did you ever dream of going to the Olympics?"

Felice "Yeah, always. I dreamed of it every day, because I used to be a competitive swimmer."

Phil "And?"

Felice "I won a few events when I was younger. And I trained and trained."

Phil "And?"

Felice "Well, by the time I turned 17, I still thought I could make it."

Phil "And?"

Felice "So, 15 years later I made it to the 2000 Olympic Games in Sydney."

Phil "Really? Unreal! What event?"

Felice "The spectator event."

BOYS RULE!
What a Laugh!

Q How many people can you fit into an empty Olympic stadium?

A One—after that it's not empty.

BOYS RULE!

| Gone Fishing | The Tree House | Golf Legends | Camping Out | Bike Daredevils |

| Water Rats | Skateboard Dudes | Tennis Ace | Basketball Buddies | Secret Agent Heroes |

| Wet World | Rock Star | Pirate Attack | Olympic Champions | Race Car Dreamers |

| Hit the Beach | Rotten School Day | Halloween Gotcha! | Battle of the Games | On the Farm |